GCSE REVIS NOTES FOR ROBERT CORMIER'S *HEROES* - Study guide (All chapters, page-by-page analysis)

by Joe Broadfoot

The right of Joe Broadfoot to be identified as the author of this work has been asserted in accordance with Section 77 of the Copyright, Designs and Patents Act 1988

ISBN 10: 1499288565

ISBN 13: 9781499288568

<u>Brief Introduction</u>

This book is aimed at GCSE students of English Literature who are studying Robert Cormier's *Heroes*. The focus is on what examiners are looking for and here you will find each chapter covered in detail. I hope this will help you and be a valuable tool in your studies and revision.

Criteria for high marks

Make sure you use appropriate critical language (see glossary of literary terms at the back). You need your argument to be fluent, well-structured and coherent. Stay focused!

Analyse and explore the use of form, structure and the language. Explore how these aspects affect the meaning.

Make connections between texts and look at different interpretations. Explore their strengths and weaknesses. Don't forget to use supporting references to strengthen your argument.

Analyse and explore the context.

Best essay practice

Use PEE for your paragraphs: point/evidence/explain.

Other tips

Make your studies active!

Don't just sit there reading! Never forget to annotate, annotate and annotate!

All page references refer to the 1999 edition published by Puffin Books (ISBN-13 978-0-14-130200-3).

Heroes

WJEC Unit 2a

If you're studying with WJEC, there's a good chance your teachers will choose this text to study. There are good reasons for that: it's moralistic and popular with students. The text encourages us to think about right and wrong. It also makes us consider the dangers of naiveté and trusting in charismatic people, who are not all that they seem. Perhaps that is why **characterisation** is virtually guaranteed to be one of the questions on the exam paper.

Chapter 1

One thing you might want to do as you complete reading each chapter is name it. This will be valuable for your revision, as you it will help you remember the plot. As well as that, you might want to reflect on why Cormier has not given the chapters titles. Could it be that he wants them to remain nameless, a bit like his protagonist: Francis Joseph Cassavant.

Incidentally, if I was to name the chapter, I would call it 'The Homecoming', as Cassavant is returning to Frenchtown after World War Two. Interestingly, Cassavant's name contains the

French word 'avant', which means 'before or after' in English. This is relevant as the narrative transports the reader backwards and forwards in time. Meanwhile, 'Cass' could refer to 'casa', which is Spanish for home. There is a certain irony in that, as Cassavant is effectively homeless in his hometown, until he finds lodgings with Mrs Belander. More about that later!

Let's continue to focus on Cassavant for now. His first name is Francis, which may remind the reader of St Francis of Assissi, who like his namesake fought in a war. Later the aforementioned saint embarked on a holy mission, whereas Cassavant's mission is for retributive justice: the killing of Larry Lasalle to avenge the rape of Nicole Renard. We don't find that out in chapter one, but we do get a sense that Cassavant is driven to do something drastic when he tells the reader: 'I thought of the gun hidden away in my duffel bag and knew that my mission was about to begin' (5).

Cassavant's middle name, 'Joseph', is harder to explain. Given the number of religious references throughout the novella, it is likely that it refers to the Biblical Joseph, who had the coat of many colours. That Biblical Joseph was the victim of jealous brothers and a rape allegation, both of which touch on a **theme** that is evident in *Heroes*: misplaced trust.

Cassavant begins his narrative with a shocking revelation that he has no face' (1). This is all the more shocking, due to the immediacy of the **present tense** and a **first-person narrative**. His use of the **simple connective** 'and' shows that he is immature, poorly educated, or a simple straightforward character (1).

The next paragraph introduces us to Dr Abrams, who tries to make Cassavant 'laugh' and is clearly a positive influence on his patient (1). The name, Dr Abrams, also seems to have religious significance. Abram may refer to Abraham, the famous Biblical father. Likewise, Dr Abrams has remodeled what's left of Cassavant's face, so he could be said to be a father-figure of sorts. Cassavant has lost both his parents so Dr Abrams is an important figure in his life, who could help him to lead a more normal life despite his horrific injuries. Therefore, Dr Abrams represents **hope**.

However, Cassavant's physical condition isolates him. His disfigured appearance results in him being shunned by society. He is an outcast, due to the tendency of people to judge books by their covers. This a theme throughout the novella. This is emphasised by the fact that he describes his nostrils as 'two small caves' (1). As an outcast, he is like a cave-dweller, living in the shadows.

The other most notable feature of Cassavant's face are his cheeks. They are formed from skin 'grafted' from his thighs (1). This suggests some kind of link between sexuality and cheeks. As you read through the novella, you may notice frequent references to cheeks to indicate sexually-charged emotion. He adds that his 'thighs sting' as his 'pants rub against them' (1). Due to his appearance and his physical condition, he is unlikely to ever experience a pleasant sensation around that area, so this description highlights his **loneliness**.

Dr Abrams compares Cassavant's cheeks of the future to a 'baby's arse' (2). This indicates rebirth, and emphasises how Dr Abrams is a father figure. As well as that, it represents hope, as Cassavant may have smooth skin 'in time' (1). Meanwhile, Dr Abrams reminds Cassavant of how unattractive he is, in a joking manner.

Cassavant has clearly thought through Dr Abrams's words carefully, as his next four sentences are separated into short paragraphs. This suggests a long pause between each statement and how Cassavant has agonised and deliberated over the words. However, he admits he has not had 'much success' in adopting Dr Abrams's 'sense of humour' (2). Perhaps it is because of his unfinished business with Larry Lasalle, that we will hear about later. Cassavant's convalescence has given him plenty of time to mull over Dr Abrams's words.

While he waits for the healing to take full effect, Cassavant has thought about how to cover up his appearance. He is currently sporting a white silk scarf, 'like the aviators wore in airplanes back during the First World War' (2). This description glamorises his appearance, but he quickly dispels the myth: 'I like to think that it [the scarf] flows behind me as I walk but I guess it doesn't' (2). Harsh reality is what Cassavant is ready to face up to. He only allows himself to dream briefly.

Cassavant goes on to describe how he wears a 'Red Sox cap' on his head (2). The Red Sox are a famous baseball team from Boston and their colours, red and white, are significant for Cassavant. The red represents the blood that has flowed from his injuries, while the white represents the purity he seeks. The red dominates the white in the team's colours, suggesting that purity is facing a losing battle against 'bloody' experience. Purity is mostly represented by Nicole Renard, but Cassavant's motives are just as pure. However misguided it is, even his thirst for bloody revenge is pure, driven by his love of Nicole.

As readers, we need to look closely at how Cassavant reveals his emotions. Despite his condition, he doesn't cry. However, his 'bandage', where his nose used to be 'gets wet' (2). He adds that 'even the doctors can't figure it out', so that means it is likely to be a release of emotion rather than just a common bodily function. This gives those moments greater significance.

Grotesque similes come to the fore later, as Cassavant describes himself as 'like the Hunchback of Notre Dame' with a face 'like a gargoyle' and his 'duffel bag like a lump' on his 'back' (3). The duffel bag is a **symbol** of the guilt he feels, which we later find out is caused by his inability to prevent Larry raping Nicole. Like in Victor Hugo's novel, *The Hunchback of Notre-Dame*, the protagonist of *Heroes* is the victim of unrequited love and is shunned by society, concerned only with superficial appearances as opposed to character. Hailing from Frenchtown, it is easy why Cassavant choses to identify himself with a disfigured character from a French novel.

Like Quasimodo from *The Hunchback of Notre-Dame*, Cassavant is viewed with 'suspicion' by other characters (3). The first character we meet is Mrs Belander, who doesn't see through Cassavant's disguise. Nothing is clear as a bell to her, so there might be some irony in her name, which sounds like a bell. It could also refer to feminine beauty, as the French word for that is 'belle'. However, 'her small black eyes' show Mrs Belander in a less flattering light (3). Perhaps her beauty has faded with old age as her 'blue veins in her legs bulging like worms beneath her skin' seem to indicate (4). Although experience seems to have hardened her, her 'face' softens and she calls Cassavant a 'poor boy' (4). This shows she has sympathy for his plight despite her suspicions.

You could say that Cassavant's future prospects are so bleak, due his injuries, that all his hopes have been dashed. This is emphasised by the mention of 'St Jude's Church', visible from his window (4). St Jude is the Catholic patron saint of desperate cases and hopeless causes. This saint advocates the virtue of perseverance and a never-say-die attitude. In regard to his mission at least, Cassavant shows the above virtues.

He also has the ability to take advice from other, as he shows by remembering Enrico Rucelli saying 'money talks' (4). The **personification** emphasises the importance of money, while the name 'Enrico' ties in with that theory, as 'rico' means 'rich' in Spanish. Financial clout is important to Enrico, who already appears to be cynical and worldly-wise. This is in sharp contrast to the more immature and naive Cassavant, who is sleeping in 'a cot' at Mrs Belander's: it seems he has still not completely grown up.

We next discover the love of Cassavant's life: Nicole Renard. The word 'renard' means 'fox', so Nicole may be expected to have similar characteristics. Perhaps we can expect Nicole to be smart and cunning like a archetypal fox. She's constantly on Cassavant's mind, as he admits he hasn't thought of her for 'maybe two hours' (4). Nicole is clearly an **obsession** for him.

We also get our first glimpse of the Wreck Centre, with its 'slanted roof' (4). It sounds quite **ominous**, as while the literal meaning of 'slanted' is that the roof is leaning in a particular direction, another connotation is that information from that building will be presented in a skewed or biased way. This, of course, is relevant given what happens there later.

You get a sense that Cassavant may be in line for a Jesus-like resurrection, as Mrs Belander demands money, 'pink palm turned upwards' (4). Given the **religious language** so far, Palm Sunday comes to mind, when Jesus was warmly welcomed to Jerusalem. This contrasts with Cassavant's frosty welcome to life back in his original hometown. The alliteration of 'pink palm' draws attention to each word. The 'palm' may refer to the tree of the same name, thus **symbolising** triumph and victory over death. Meanwhile, the pink of Mrs Belander's skin reminds us of Cassavant's horrific injuries.

We discover that Mrs Belander 'had always been generous' and baked Cassavant a cake on his 'thirteenth birthday', five years ago (4). Not only do we find out that she is warm-hearted, but we also notice Cassavant's sentimentality as his 'caves moistened' highlighting his emotional distress. This is also brought on by the 'red-and-white checked oilcloth' that reminds him of home (4). In short, he is a sentimental character.

Cassavant is happy to remain **anonymous**, saying it's 'fine' with him when Mrs Belander writes '*Tenant*' where his name should be on his receipt (4). She still remains a kind person, which is proven when she offers him 'sturdy soup' despite some lingering 'suspicion' (5).

St Jude's Church is the next scene as Cassavant enters and lights a candle. He reminisces about his days as an altar boy for Father Balthazar, who shares the same name as one of the three wise men who visited the Baby Jesus bearing gifts. Presumably, Cassavant gained as good deal of religious **wisdom** from Balthazar, although he struggled to remember 'Latin responses' (5).

Enrico, missing two legs and a left arms, is in Cassavant's thoughts, and he reflects on his friend's joke: 'Thank God I'm right-handed' (5). There may be sexual significance in that statement as his injuries mean he is unlikely to achieve union with another and may have to rely on self-stimulation. This highlights the character's desperate plight and **loneliness**.

After he has finished praying for Enrico, Cassavant prays for his dead 'mother and father' (5). His status as an orphan evokes even more **sympathy** from the reader. He prays for his Uncle Louis and Nicole before finishing his prayers with Larry, the man he is 'going to kill' (6). He says it fills him with 'guilt and shame', but he wants to adhere to what he was taught by Sister Gertrude, which is to 'pray for his enemies' (6). It shows the importance of religion in Cassavant's life and how his **faith** is unshaken by his bitter experiences.

We later hear how Dr Abrams claims he can improve Cassavant's life. Abrams is moving his practice to Kansas City, which seems to link him with L. Frank Baum's novel, *The Wonderful Wizard of Oz*. The fictional character of the wizard offered improbable solution to the other characters' problems, but by contrast, 'cosmetic surgery' may provide a real answer to Cassavant's (6). Enrico thinks Abrams's should operate on himself to make himself look less 'like Abraham Lincoln' (7). Interestingly, Lincoln was assassinated, which is what Cassavant intends to do to Larry. The discussion about cosmetic surgery links to the novella's **theme** of deceiving appearances.

The sound of Enrico's laugh is 'like a saw going through wood' (7). This reminds us that Enrico's legs and one arms have been amputated and possibly sawn off. The simile graphically reminds the reader of the horrors of war.

Enrico calls Cassavant a 'big hero' and a 'Silver Star hero' (7). Modestly, Cassavant denies that he deserves that tag. As readers, we begin to wonder how the protagonist defines a hero, given that he disagrees with his friend.

Chapter 2

Although Cassavant worships God, he also prostrates himself in front of Nicole. When he sees her for the first time, he is kneeling 'on the floor' (9). This is significant, as he puts her on a pedestal.

He goes on to describe her as 'small and slender, with shining black hair' (9). He compares the 'pale purity of her face' to a statue of St Therese, a popular Roman Catholic saint like St Francis (9). Therese hated pretence, so it is ironic that Larry, who is not all that he seems, becomes her nemesis later in the novella.

However, Nicole is not as pure as Therese. The narrator notes that 'a hint of mischief' flashed in her eyes, 'as if she were telling me we were going to have good times together' (9). These words give the reader the impression that Nicole is flirtatious. Nevertheless, Cassavant continues to put her on a pedestal, describing her 'sword' touching his shoulder as he 'knelt there like a knight' (10). Although he pledges 'his love and loyalty for ever', he is unable to protect her from the unsavoury fate that awaits her (10). This failure on his part to live up to his own chivalric ideals is the source of his **guilt**. Yet, Nicole 'ignored' him, so it's hard to understand why he's fallen so madly in love with this aloof tease.

Cassavant's feeling of inferiority to Nicole is highlighted by her address: she lives in 'Sixth', while he lives in 'Fifth Street' (10). This subtly suggests that is she is numerically above him. Even Nicole's friend, Marie LeCroix, 'lived above' Cassavant (10). LeCroix translates as 'the cross', which once again gives Nicole and her friend religious significance. It's as if they are meant to be worshipped.

Cassavant describes how he 'lurked on the piazza below', when Nicole visits Marie (10). This foreshadows Cassavant's fate as a person on the fringes of society, who can only lurk around others due to his horrific injuries. He describes himself 'like a sentry on lonely guard duty', which makes it seem he was always destined for a lonely life and entry to the armed services.

Marie seems completely different to Nicole. She seems coarse and vulgar, in comparison to the seemingly perfect Nicole. Marie reveals that Sister Mathilde 'lets off her farts in the corridor' (11). The contrast between Marie and Nicole highlights the latter's purity. However, it may be that Nicole's distance from Cassavant allows him to project his ideals on a blank canvass, so to speak. The fact that she associates with Marie suggests she may not be quite as different from her as she seems on the surface. Appearances can be deceiving, as we find out later with Larry.

Colour creeps into Cassavant's 'cheeks', as he reveals his affection for Nicole (11). These same cheeks are now skin-grafted from his thighs, so it reminds the reader of Cassavant's injuries. He describes his cheeks 'incinerating', as Marie asks him questions about his love for Nicole (12). This burning sensation reminds the reader that Cassavant's love for her has led to him living in a self-inflicted hell.

Cassavant later lives in a similar state to the protagonist of Ernest Hemingway's *The Sun Also Rises*, who is also a victim of war and disappointed by the love of his life. It is no coincidence that Cassavant is 'reading' this novel, while Marie and Nicole converse one floor above him (11).

We also get the feeling that Cassavant is cursed, as he hears his father saying that 'selling Babe Ruth to the Yankees brought a curse upon' the Red Sox (12). Cassavant wears a Red Sox cap, which shows he's as cursed as the team. It seems to be self-inflicted curse though, as he doesn't have to wear it. Meanwhile, 'Babe Ruth' conjures up images of babies and **naiveté**, which is Cassavant's Achilles heel (12).

Joey LeBlanc is another character we meet in this chapter. He seems to be a male version of Marie LeCroix, given his crudity. His surname, LeBlanc, like LeCroix's, belies his attitude. 'Blanc' means 'white' in French, but Joey is far from pure. He calls out to Nicole, whose 'white dress' is a 'blur', suggesting that she is not all she seems (13). Joey's comment about a 'run' in her 'stocking', sexualises Nicole somewhat (14). This hints at the sexual abuse she is later to endure. In comparison to Joey, Cassavant lacks **confidence** as he doesn't know who Nicole had been 'waving at'.

Chapter 3

Vivid imagery begins the chapter, as the narrator describes Mr Molnier's 'blood-stained apron', and 'white curtains' Nicole's old apartment (15). Once again, the colours red and white predominate. Red reminds us of how Cassavant's body has been butchered, while the white reminds us of Nicole's purity of yesteryear.

We meet Norman Rocheleau, who shares the same initials as Nicole. Like Cassavant, he has a penchant for reading. Norman swaps his 'military edition of *The Great Gatsby*' for a pack of cigarettes (16). Through F. Scott Fitzgerald's novel, we get a reference to a doomed protagonist, who is obsessively in love. As readers, we feel that Cassavant is just as unlikely to achieve his romantic goal as Gatsby.

Cassavant reveals to Norman that Nicole's 'cologne' was 'like spring flowers that always clung to her' (17). Yet he remembers walking down 'Mechanic Street' with her, which does not evoke such romantic imagery. The reader gets the idea that their love will need repair work, the way a car needs a mechanic.

The colours of injury and purity are once again presented, as Cassavant reveals he has bought 'bread and strawberry jam' and Campbell's soups in the red and white cans' (18). Additionally, he mentions that he's bought 'pea soup' (18). 'Pea' is a **homophone** for the slang word 'pee', which is urine. It sounds unglamorous and especially unfitting for a hero, particularly one who has been awarded a Silver Star.

There is a sense that Cassavant is emulating Larry, his nemesis, as he deceives Mrs Belander. He admits: 'It scares me, how easy it is to lie' (19). Like Larry's lies, Cassavant's fool his victim: Mrs Belander, who replies, 'Poor boy' (18).

Cassavant wants to remember the true heroes of his 'platoon' (20). Before sleeping, he recites 'the names of the guys'. It's a religious ritual, as he compares it to 'a litany, the names of the

GIs like beads on a rosary' (20). These names will be forgotten; but Cassavant's sense of justice sees him try desperately to cling on to memories of the heroes, despite wanting 'to forget what happened there in France' (20).

Red and white are the dominant colours in a dream, as Cassavant describes 'two German soldiers in white uniforms' and the head of one of them exploding 'like a ripe tomato' (21). The other soldier 'cries *Mama*', which reminds us that his is another young life wasted (21). The white uniforms suggest innocence, while the tomato, presumably red, obviously refers to the indiscriminate bloodshed.

Then Cassavant compares his dream to reality. The tomato simile is an exaggeration, but the grim truth is just as graphic as he reveals 'how young they were, boys with apple cheeks' (22). Once again, Cassavant refers to cheeks as a measure of age and experience.

Chapter 4

We meet Arthur Rivier looking at Cassavant 'curiously' and 'with sympathy' (23). Cassavant claims he is 'not deserving' of sympathy, so this makes us question his reliability as a narrator. Meanwhile, we discover that Arthur was a sporting hero before entering the army , as 'a star first baseman for the Frenchtown Tigers' (23). Now his eyes are 'bleary and bloodshot'; the alliteration reminds us of his poor physical state due to the effects of alcohol (23). Heroism and stardom seems to have reduced him to this.

Nevertheless, Cassavant reveals how 'impatient' he was 'to reach the age when' he could join his heroes 'in that great crusade for freedom' (24). This shows how he attributes religious significance to the war effort. He seems desperate to find a cause to attach himself to, whether it be defending Nicole's honour or his country's interests.

There is more evidence that joining the army is a mistake, as Big Boy Burgeron reveals 'the infantry spoiled' his feet (25). By contrast, Cassavant has suffered a lot more than Big Boy, so this comment emphasises the protagonist's dreadful predicament.

Despite his silence, Arthur shows Cassavant respect, saying: 'You earned the right not to talk' (26). This indicates that the walking wounded are held in high regard for their exploits, despite injuries causing low self-esteem. In Cassavant's case, he still seem to see himself as 'little' and has not completely grown up yet (26). Perhaps that's why, he cannot believe he deserves the status of a hero.

Chapter 5

The importance of 'The Wreck Centre' is highlighted by the use of capital letters: 'FRENCHTOWN REC. CENTRE' (27). Cassavant's emotional involvement with the place is emphasised by his physical response, evidenced when he admits: 'it's not the moisture from my caves that has dampened my scarf' (27). His connection to the place goes back to the time when it was called 'Grenier's Hall', which sounds a little like the word 'grenade' but means 'attic'. The French phrase 'de la cave au grenier' means 'high and low', which reflects Cassavant's mixed feelings for the place.

As the narrative continues, we veer away from the 'faint sickly pink', which reflects Cassavant's mixed emotions, to the distinct red and white of the place's past (27). We discover that Marie-Blanche Touraine, whose middle name means 'white', was shot down in cold blood, presumably spilling red blood on her wedding gown (28).

The 'carpenters and painters' may have tried to erase the place's troubled past with 'white paint', but it 'didn't completely cover the dark patches of mildew' (28, 29). The words 'Wreck Centre' is incorrectly emblazoned in 'bright red paint' on 'the sign' and the signals it sends out is mostly negative (29).

Out of this hell that cannot be turned into heaven, however much it's given a facelift, appears Larry LaSalle. The French word 'salle' means 'room', and this is quite appropriate given the role Cassavant's nemesis plays. 'Salle de danse' means 'dance hall' and we will later see the Wreck Centre become this. At this point, 'salle de cinema', meaning cinema, is more relevant given Larry's 'movie-star teeth' (29). Those teeth suggest that Larry is a fake. Meanwhile, Larry is shown to be multi-talented with 'the broad shoulders of an athlete and the narrow hips of a dancer' (29). In other words, Larry's identity is hard to pin down. Appearances are already deceptive, when it comes to LaSalle, who can transform himself like a room that becomes what you want it to be with a few decorations and some furniture. Ironically, one of the first things Larry says is 'it's real' (29). Although he's only referring to his name, the authenticity of Larry's personality remains in question.

The use of **antithesis** makes the reader continue to doubt Larry. Although he walks like 'Fred Astaire' with 'his feet barely touching the floor', when he tap-dances, he does it with 'machine-gun speed' (30). This last metaphor suggests that he makes holes in the floor with his dancing feet, and this image certainly conveys a strong sense of danger represented by Larry.

LaSalle appears to be a Jesus Christ-like character; however, instead of turning water into wine, Larry shows how 'old wine jugs' can be transformed 'into lamps' (31). Perhaps he is an anti-Christ, as he's turning something that contained wine, representing the blood of Christ, into something that can burn, like the fires of Hell.

Nicole appears soon after LaSalle in the narrative, with her supposed purity emphasised by the whiteness of her appearance. Cassavant catches 'flashes of her white thighs' and notes the 'drops of perspiration on her forehead like raindrops on white porcelain' (32). This description eroticises Nicole somewhat, which negates her virginal image.

The final thought in the chapter gives the reader the idea that Joey LeBlanc is often right. Joey predicts that only 'Doom' awaits the Wreck Centre and, with hindsight, Cassavant admits that prediction was correct (33). Cassavant reveals that Joey died fighting the Japanese on the island of 'Iwo

Jima', where some of the resistance forces retired underground into caves to avoid defeat (33). It is reminiscent of Cassavant's caves, as he endures suffering in an attempt to complete his mission.

Chapter 6

The narrative reaches the month of April and the weather reflects the protagonist's mood when he states that: 'the clouds are still thick and low, and the rain falls almost every day' (34). The rain in the description makes Cassavant sound miserable, while the clouds suggest he is still burdened by his unresolved mission. A clearer sky might indicate some kind of break through. Please note, this is **not** an example of pathetic fallacy. If the clouds were frowning and the rain were whipping him, for example, then it would be an example pathetic fallacy, as the elements would be taking on human attributes. Let's not forget, pathetic fallacy is a form of personification (see glossary at the end of this book).

The focus shifts to other characters, as Cassavant notes Arthur's mouth 'twitching' as if 'tugged by invisible fingers' (35). Cassavant is like an invisible man, given his attire, but the salient point is these heroes are showing signs of physical frailty. Even the baseball superstar mentioned, 'Lou Gehrig', suffered from motor neurone disease in later life (35). The narrative suggests that heroism, if achievable, is only temporary.

Meanwhile, Larry's status as a cult hero remains intact. The almost religious devotion of his followers is spelt out by Arthur, who raises a glass to make a toast to: 'the patron saint of the Wreck Centre' (36). Even the bar tender, the old Strangler, pours 'himself a glass of red wine', which suggests a religious service when participants drink the blood of Christ (36).

Interestingly, the Strangler reveals that Larry's Silver Star was for 'gallantry' (37). This word has chivalric nuances, relating to knights' behaviour towards damsels in distress, and is completely inappropriate given Larry's alleged serial sexual abuse of women. Therefore, the word is **ironic**.

Meanwhile, perhaps for the first time, we get a sense of Cassavant's lingering pride in his own sporting achievments. Although Cassavant insists on Arthur not making a 'fuss', when it comes to recognising his Silver Star for bravery, he is quick to remind him that he was 'table tennis champion', rather than a 'champ' at 'ping-pong' (37, 38). This pedantry shows that Cassavant has some fond memories of the Wreck Centre, where he first began to believe in his own ability.

Chapter 7

The positive influence Larry initially had on Cassavant is revealed early on in this chapter. The protagonist bemoans his lack of talent when he tells Larry: 'I'm rotten at everything' (39). Larry replies by telling Cassavant that he has 'outstanding reflexes' (39). Larry improves Cassavant's sense of self-worth so, in this respect, his nemesis has had a positive effect on him. Therefore, it would be wrong to dismiss Larry as a completely evil character, as he does have a good side.

The pedantic Larry explains to Cassavant the difference between ping-pong and table tennis and, as we saw in a previous chapter, this pedantry has been adopted by his protégé. Larry says: 'Ping-pong is a game, table tennis is a sport' (40). This is important, as being a former table tennis champion is the only thing that Cassavant is proud of. The ball makes a 'satisfying *plop*' sound, which deglamorises it somewhat, given its possible association with lavatory noises (40).

Although Larry's influence on Cassavant seems entirely positive, at this stage, the language used suggests that LaSalle could be a sinister character. The narrative reveals that Larry 'lured awkward girls into ballet classes' (41). The word 'lured' suggests that Larry's intent is not altogether pure.

Larry's intentions for Nicole seem particularly impure. Cassavant recognises this as he admits feeling jealous as Larry gets 'only an inch or so from a kiss' with Nicole during a dance class (42). It seems as if Larry is abusing his position of power over Nicole, who is portrayed prostrate laying 'at his feet' (42). Although it's just a dance routine, it has greater significance than that. The sinister undertones of the song title, 'Dancing in the Dark', which they're dancing to, suggests danger (42). This danger is fully realised later in the novella, when we discover Larry's fatal flaw that prevents him from being a hero in the truest sense of the word.

We get an indication of how Cassavant pictures a true hero, when he imagines himself accepting a trophy for table tennis 'with the modesty of a true champion' (43). Interestingly, he imagines that the trophy will be 'silver', which is the colour of the star he later receives for bravery (43). There is something chivalric is how Cassavant imagines Nicole handing him the trophy, as if he is her gallant knight. Table tennis appears to be a modern form of jousting in the novella.

This sport makes Cassavant feel good about himself, especially as it results in Nicole complimenting him. Using sea imagery, the narrator admits: 'a tide of confidence swept through me' (44). It implies, that like a tide, that confidence will ebb and flow.

Nicole's intimacy with Larry is considered, as the narrator reveals that she calls LaSalle '"Larry", spoken off-hand as if they were more than teacher and pupil' (44). Her words fill him with mixed emotions, 'delight and agony' (44). The suggestion is the result of this relationship will be pain, as Cassavant reveals: 'my flesh burned with the echo of her touch' (44). This figurative language highlights the fate that awaits him, as he will be suffering from the burning sensations caused by his physical injuries and inhabiting a psychological hell upon his return to his hometown.

However, this chapter relives the good times. Louis Arabelle is pitted against Cassavant in the table tennis championship. Interestingly, Louis's name is quite similar to Larry's, sharing a lot of the same letters. Louis plays a 'deceptive game', but Cassavant effectively deals with his 'soft strokes and dizzy spins' (45). Unfortunately, he is unable to handle Larry's deception later in the novella.

As Cassavant prepares to take on Larry at table tennis, he notices 'Nicole beside him' (46). This does not augur well for Cassavant's future with her, although he enjoys 'the radiance of her face mirroring his own' (46). It is interesting that Joey calls Larry 'Mister LaSalle', unlike Nicole who is on first-name terms with her teacher (46). Once again, intimacy between the two of them is being strongly hinted at.

Once the game takes place, Cassavant suspects that Larry is 'letting' him win, 'feigning frustration' (47). The alliteration emphasises how underhanded, which is how table tennis is best played, Larry is being. The question is, though, how reliable is the narrator? It could be his natural modesty that is preventing Cassavant from recognising his own talent.

Cassavant's nemesis finally starts to live up to his billing as an enemy, as Larry is described with 'narrowed eyes', which are 'inscrutable' and 'mysterious' (48).

Chapter 8

Arthur's drunkenness is highlighted and it is no accident that he is portrayed 'slumped' at 'the entrance to Pee Alley'; this location implies that the place is a place to urinate for drunks (49). The 'dribbles of saliva on his lips and chin' ensure he is portrayed in an unflattering light (49). He lives in the past, as he wants to talk about the 'war', as opposed to some veterans' future prospects of 'going to college' (49).

Arthur calls the war 'sacred', giving it religious significance (50). However, he affords it no glamour as he admits he 'messed' his 'pants' (50). Armand feels sorry for Arthur, but Cassavant pities all of them that took part in the war. The harshness of the environment the veterans are in is emphasised by the **personification** of the wind. Using **pathetic fallacy**, the narrator reveals that the 'cold wind buffets the buildings' making the veterans' plight seem all the more desperate (50).

Chapter 9

Although at time, Larry has been portrayed in a slightly sinister light prior to this chapter, this is not the case in the opening of this one. Riding on the crest of war-fever, he plays the crowd-pleaser with consummate ease. He seems so genuine, appearing with 'the movie-star smile gone, replaced by grim-faced determination' (51). Like Cassavant, Larry appears to be modest. Rather than accepting the adulation of the adoring crowd, Larry holds 'up his hand' and tells them: 'None of that, kids. I'm just doing what millions of others are doing' (51). Although, he is downplaying his contribution to the war effort, the effect is to make what he is doing all the more impressive.

The message is that war can seem glamorous, especially when you're on the outside looking in. Everybody was willing to play their part, even Cassavant's Uncle Louis, who was rumoured to be 'producing secret material' for the war effort (52). Cassavant wants to know if this is true, but his uncle replies: 'Shhhh! (52)' This reinforces the idea that secret activities are going on at the Monument Comb Factory, despite Uncle Louis previously admitting to only making 'combs and brushes, knives and forks' (52). Cassavant's gullibility makes him believe the more glamorous notion, which appeals to his sense of family pride and patriotism.

The backdrop of war can be a romantic setting, as Ernest Hemingway discovered when he wrote the best seller 'A Farewell To Arms', which both Cassavant and Nicole enjoy reading. Books draw them closer together, as do movies (53). She even gives him a 'Butterscotch Bit', which hints at greater intimacy to come (53).

However, Nicole remains slightly aloof. She insists 'on buying her own' movie-theatre ticket and her hand stays 'cool' in Cassavant's, despite him profusely sweating (53, 54). She allows him an 'innocent kiss' with their 'lips briefly touching' (54). Even Cassavant admits 'she had a way of teasing', which suggests she doesn't take his love seriously (54).

Nicole takes the war effort seriously, though, and wants to 'help more' (55). Cassavant teases her immaturely, suggesting she smells of 'cooked cabbage' from all the time she spends in the convent, knitting for the armed forces (55). Nicole shows a greater maturity, by replying that it's 'better than' a popular perfume called 'Evening in Paris' (55). This shows Nicole is unimpressed with cosmetic smells and wants to make a real difference to the war effort, no matter how unglamorous cabbage smells.

Although Cassavant tries to make light of the '7 December party', by singing '"Dancing in the Dark" in a comic way', Nicole remembers it as 'a sad party' (55). That was the day when the Japanese attacked Pearl Harbour and Cassavant and Nicole discovered 'the world was not a safe place anymore' (55). Clearly, Larry's surprise attack on Nicole, which happens later, can be likened to the aforementioned bombing on 7th December 1941. This comparison is made even stronger by the same song playing each time terrible events come to light.

However, at this point in the narrative, Larry is everyone's hero. Nicole seems particularly impressed by Larry's exploits, asking 'breathlessly' if Cassavant has heard the news (56). The word 'breathlessly' suggests she feels some attraction towards Larry.

When Larry appears on the 'Movietone News', he appears very real: 'unshaven, face gaunt and drawn, eyes sunk deep into their sockets' (56). He appears to have suffered a lot for his country, and seems to deserve the title of 'the town's first big war hero on the silver screen' (57).

Chapter 10

We get a sense of the slightly masochist nature of Cassavant's personality, when he states: 'I enjoyed the sting of air on my flesh' (58). The 'bright sunshine' disappoints him, and he seems prefer the mystery of 'stalking through the shadows' (58). In a matter-of-fact manner, he graphically describes his nose as 'like the snout of an animal', as he realises his appearance is now horrifying to others (58). These quotations show how mentally strong Cassavant is, as he does not seem particularly fazed by his new appearance. Indeed, his biggest complaint is about the sunny weather, initially.

Later, Cassavant explains how he got 'the white scarf' (59). Enrico won it in a 'poker game', so this suggests that the scarf may bring out the gambler in Cassavant, who is betting on his ability to kill Larry and remain largely unidentified (59). Like the wounds of his psychological injury inflicted by Larry, Cassavant's cheeks remain 'raw and red' (59). It seems as if he won't be able to heal until his 'mission', a word which has religious connotations, is completed (59).

However, it appears that like Enrico, Cassavant is planning his own demise. The word 'disposal' is used as a euphemism for the suicide both of them are contemplating (59). Suicide would mean being barred from heaven, so it seems apt that the protagonist watches 'the flames eating up the list of hospitals' where Enrico might be (60). Cassavant seems ready to embrace an afterlife of hell.

Chapter 11

As he awaits the return of Larry, Cassavant describes his nemesis as 'a bright Pied Piper' (61). Like that legendary character who initially rids Hamelin of rats, Larry does the Frenchtown a good deed, before spoiling all his good work upon his return. Sound imagery heralds Larry's arrival, as the narrator notes the 'hiss of steam' from the train (61). This use of personification emphasises the danger represented by Larry, as the 'hiss' announcing his arrival reminds the reader of a snake and therefore deception.

Indeed, Larry appears even more dangerous than before with his 'knife-like' and 'lethal' slenderness (62). Larry's feeling for Nicole seems obvious given 'the rush of affection on his face' (62). The feeling seems mutual seeing as Nicole's blush turns 'her cheeks crimson' (62). You get the feeling that cheeks don't lie in this novella! Additionally, her blood is clearly pumping through her veins for Larry, which is in stark contrast to the cold hands she has when Cassavant holds them.

Larry appears to be the epitome of unselfish heroism, when he 'modestly' accepts the 'silver key to the city' (63). Later we find out his words are **ironic**, when he says: 'We have to keep the world safe for these young people' (63). Obviously, he abuses the trust invested in him, by sexually abusing Nicole. Rather than making the world a safe place for her, he has turned it into a more dangerous place by returning. However, at this stage, she is unaware of the risk he poses.

The language leaves us in no doubt that looks are deceptive, as Larry leads them in 'a wild snake dance through Monument Square' (64). Nicole has 'her hands' on Larry's 'hips', which suggests that the 'surprise' awaiting her may be less-than-innocent (64).

Perhaps Nicole feels some attraction towards Larry, as she's been watching him being embraced by 'beautiful women' .

Just after that she is described as 'wide-eyed and wistful', which suggests she's innocently longing for something she can't have: in other words, Larry. She seems to want to emulate a woman wearing 'a simple white gown that clung to her body like whipped cream' (64). It seems as if she longs to be like one of the beautiful women hugging Larry.

Meanwhile, the returning hero, Larry, calls his medals and ribbons 'scrambled eggs' (65). This indicates that he has killed a lot of young things to get those accolades, as you can't scramble eggs without breaking eggs. Those eggs, of course, represent young lives. Nicole is instinctively right to tell Cassavant to 'stay close', given the danger she is in, unbeknown to her (65).

Her instincts strengthen as she commands Cassavant to 'stay and watch', as she begins dancing with Larry (66). Cassavant trusts his mentor enough to do exactly what Larry suggests instead. He even seems 'actually to be tired', so strong is Larry's power of suggestion (66). Larry appears to have a devil's power at this point.

The 'plop' noise of the record falling on the platter is reminiscent of the 'plop' of the table tennis ball earlier, which signalled Cassavant's proudest moment (67). Now the same sound marks the depths of his despair. The 'scratching of the needle' suggests an act of violence has taken place in the darkness: Nicole has been violated (67).

She is then described 'whimpering, like a small animal caught and trapped' (68). This shows how defenceless she really is.

Nicole needed Cassavant to defend her like a knight in shining armour, but he let her down.

Larry continues to appear as a diabolical character, looking like a 'ghostly silhouette' (69). He turns into a 'shadow' and his callous nature is revealed as Cassavant hears him 'whistling a tune' (69). Although Larry whistles 'softly', it belies the nature of the act he has just committed.

Chapter 12

Like Larry, Cassavant turns into a ghost of sorts, as he admits he 'haunted Sixth Street at all hours' (70). Despite his dedication, he doesn't see Nicole. The 'heat wave' suggests he is inhabiting a hell on earth. The heat is emphasised by personification, as the narrative revealed it 'gripped Frenchtown' (70). This makes the oppressive heat sound even more alarming.

Cassavant admits 'it was part of the hell' that he 'had earned', but he is not a devil like Larry (71). However, when a small boy asks him if he is 'the bogey man', he is tempted to say he is (70). The guilt he feels at letting Larry rape 'his girl' makes him feel he deserves the 'bogey man' title (71).

Like the small boy, Nicole condemns Cassavant with 'accusation in her voice' (72). Furthermore, the antithesis in her speech reveals her confusion, as she calls Cassavant 'poor', yet 'with no pity in her voice' (72). Cassavant feels doomed as there seems to be 'no forgiveness' for his 'sins'

(72). Once again, there are strong religious connotations in the narrative.

As Cassavant climbs the steep stairs of the Father Balthazar's church, his breath comes 'in gasps, the sound like cloth ripping' (73). It is impossible not to think of the rape scene given that imagery. He is certainly seeking refuge in heaven, hoping to dispel his sins from his mind. The imagery evoked suggests that this attempt is unsuccessful.

While up there, Cassavant contemplates suicide. He is ashamed of himself at the thought. He decides he wants to die 'with honour' on battlefield (74). Once again, he has decided to try to do the honourable thing, like a knight in shining armour. Later chronologically and also like a knight, Cassavant wears a scarf. Knights used to wear the scarves, veils or sleeves of the lady they were jousting for. Therefore, it's interesting that when Cassavant reappears in Frenchtown he's wearing a white scarf: undoubtedly the colour most associated with Nicole.

Chapter 13

Cassavant has to live with his guilt and while he waits exact revenge, he is 'stunned' to hear Mrs Belander and Mrs Agneaux discussing Larry (75). They had just been discussing Mr Tardier, who is fond of pinching 'women on the *derriere* when they pass', so the close juxtaposition of the two names suggests that Larry is just as creepy (75).

However, Mrs Agneaux reveals that Larry's 'legs hurt' (76). He is living in a 'green house', which may represent 'fading' innocence (76). The paint is 'cheap', a bit like Larry's trick to make Cassavant leave the hall so he could commit his heinous act (76).

Chapter 14

The chapter starts with a striking simile comparing Cassavant's weapon to cancer: 'The gun is like a tumour on my thigh' (77). Like cancer, the desire to fire the weapon has been eating away at him. The desire for revenge seems to be slowly killing him from within.

However, his nemesis has changed. Larry 'seems fragile' now, so perhaps worthy of pity (78). Interestingly, he is located by 'the black coal stove', which conjures up images of burning in Hell (78).

While at Larry's though, Cassavant experiences a rare cold sensation, 'as if winter has invaded' his bones' (79). It's as if he suddenly regrets his mission. The hot passion that is fuelling has momentarily left him.

His urge to kill Larry returns, as he refers to him as 'a fake' (80). Using a euphemism, he relates that he wants to 'rid' himself 'of the fakery' (80). In other words, he wants to kill Larry still. The present tense heightens the immediacy and tension produced by this encounter.

Although Larry is shocked by Cassavant's revelation that he knows about Nicole, he still calmly tries to justify his crime. Larry tells Cassavant: 'The sweet young things, Francis. Even their heat is sweet. . . (81)'. It seems likely that Larry has preyed on more than just Nicole, given that he's referred to 'things' in plural. The words 'heat' and 'sweet' rhyme, drawing attention to both. The word 'heat' seems to mean sexuality, but it also is suggestive of the hell that Larry has created.

Larry's diabolical nature comes to the fore as he reveals: 'We love the thing that makes us evil' (82). Yet, he also seems more fragile now than he was, with 'his lips trembling' and his legs useless (82). It would be dishonourable to kill Larry in this condition, so we can hardly expect Cassavant to pull the trigger.

Larry's piteous state is further exemplified by his 'voice' as he begs Cassavant, 'like the small cry of a child' (83). The hell that Larry inhabits is 'too warm' for Cassavant, who wants to leave without completing his mission (83). Once again, he has broken a pledge. Before he promised not to leave Nicole's side, yet he allowed her to be raped. Now he's ready to give up on his mission to kill her rapist.

As Cassavant hears Larry shoot himself, he is reminded of the sound 'of a ping-pong ball striking the table' (84). Interestingly, he has stopped referring to the sport as table tennis. It is a dishonourable game now, instead.

Chapter 15

Another sound begins the next chapter, as we hear a 'doorbell' echoing 'through the long corridors of the convent' (85). The familiar smell of 'cabbage' greets Cassavant as he encounters a nun. The implication is that nuns are far more like heroes and contribute more to humanity than those perfume-wearing girls that Cassavant used to serve in the shop.

When he finally meets Sister Mathilde, she says: 'I heard you served your country well' (86). As well as his country, Cassavant has been serving table tennis balls and customers earlier in the novella. He seems born to serve. His natural modesty showed him to be happy to retrieve baseballs as a child and he seems always willing to put himself at somebody else's disposal. Of course, 'disposal' is another key word in the text, given the way it was used as a euphemism earlier.

Cassavant contines his discussion with the nun, 'glad that he face is behind the scarf and the bandage' (87). In a sense, he is being hypocritical, as he accused Larry of being a 'fake' and now he is engaging in a similar amount of deception. However, it could be said that Cassavant is only guilty of white lies.

There is also another sense that Cassavant is not so unlike Larry after all, as he seems to get a perverse thrill out of touching 'a nun's flesh' (88). He also wonders if it is 'a special sin to lie to a nun' (88). His conscience is racked with guilt, but he keeps on lying regardless.

Chapter 16

Like Larry's house, Nicole's cardigan is 'green' (89). Also like Larry her appearance has changed, as she bears the brunt of the rape. There is no sign of 'that glimpse of mischief' that she used to have in her eyes (89). She seems to be a shell of her former self.

The colour green returns as the narrator briefly describes the 'fields' and 'the tennis court' (90). Tennis could be considered to be the much more honourable version of ping-pong, and therefore that makes Cassavant appear completely out of his depth in these surroundings. He seems inadequate, although Nicole forgives him for his sins by saying he wasn't 'to blame' (90).

Cassavant focuses on 'the plopping' of a tennis ball outside, as he compares it to ping-pong (91). The tennis ball 'doesn't have the sharp sound of a ping-pong ball on a table. Or a gun shot' (91). Through this imagery, you get a sense that Nicole is in a much safer place now.

However, Nicole seems more fake now than she once was. Although she has a 'bright smile on her face', it is not reflected 'in her eyes' (92). Bitter experience has hardened her.

She admits she 'couldn't help teasing' Cassavant, so she is still quite honest (93). She also admits pretending to enjoy the 'fake endings' of the movies they saw (93). Interestingly, 'she says her palm was wet, too' when they used to hold hands

(93). Perhaps she is just being kind to Cassavant, who she can see is suffering from severe facial injuries.

Before he leaves her, Cassavant admits he doesn't 'know what a hero is any more' (94). Nicole tries to give him encouragement to write about it, which shows that despite her bitterness she is still a kind person. However, she does not want to share her life with Cassavant, which is why she 'steps away' (94).

Nevertheless, she kisses the place on his scarf where his lips are. As she does so, Cassavant feels 'the pressure of her lips' (95). Likewise, it could be said that he has felt the pressure of her love and is now better off without it.

Relieved of the pressure of feeling obliged to love Nicole and avenge his rape, Cassavant is free to follow his own destiny. Perhaps he is no longer ready to serve. Instead, he sits and observes. As well as that, he reminisces. he thinks of his 'old platoon' (96). He calls them, the 'real heroes' (96). Finally, Cassavant has discovered the meaning of the word.

However, his future is still full of doubt. The repetition of the word 'maybe' indicates exactly how uncertain that future is. He seems to suddenly enjoy the weight of his duffel bag, which now feels 'nice and comfortable' (97). This shows that he has learned to live with his feelings of guilt, which are no longer burdening him. He is now free to pursue any future he wishes.

Essay writing tips

<u>Use a variety of connectives</u>

Have a look of this list of connectives. Which of these would you choose to use?

'ADDING' DISCOURSE MARKERS

- AND

- ALSO

- AS WELL AS

- MOREOVER

- TOO

- FURTHERMORE

- ADDITIONALLY

I hope you chose 'additionally', 'furthermore' and 'moreover'. Don't be afraid to use the lesser discourse markers, as they are also useful. Just avoid using those ones over and over again. I've seen essays from Key Stage 4 students that use the same discourse marker for the opening sentence of each paragraph! Needless to say, those essays didn't get great marks!

Okay, here are some more connectives for you to look at. Select the best ones.

'SEQUENCING' DISCOURSE MARKERS

- NEXT

- FIRSTLY

- SECONDLY

- THIRDLY

- FINALLY

- MEANWHILE

- AFTER

- THEN

- SUBSEQUENTLY

This time, I hope you chose 'subsequently' and 'meanwhile'.

Here are some more connectives for you to 'grade'!

'ILLUSTRATING / EXEMPLIFYING' DISCOURSE MARKERS

- FOR EXAMPLE

- SUCH AS

- FOR INSTANCE

- IN THE CASE OF

- AS REVEALED BY

- ILLUSTRATED BY

I'd probably go for 'illustrated by' or even 'as exemplified by' (which is not in the list!). Please feel free to add your own examples to the lists. Strong connectives impress examiners. Don't forget it! That's why I want you to look at some more.

'CAUSE & EFFECT' DISCOURSE MARKERS

- BECAUSE

- SO

- THEREFORE

- THUS

- CONSEQUENTLY

- HENCE

I'm going for 'consequently' this time. How about you? What about the next batch?

'COMPARING' DISCOURSE MARKERS

- SIMILARLY

- LIKEWISE

- AS WITH

- LIKE

- EQUALLY

- IN THE SAME WAY

I'd choose 'similarly' this time. Still some more to go.

'QUALIFYING' DISCOURSE MARKERS

- BUT

- HOWEVER

- WHILE

- ALTHOUGH

- UNLESS

- EXCEPT

- APART FROM

- AS LONG AS

It's 'however' for me!

'CONTRASTING' DISCOURSE MARKERS

- WHEREAS

- INSTEAD OF

- ALTERNATIVELY

- OTHERWISE

- UNLIKE

- ON THE OTHER HAND

- CONVERSELY

I'll take 'conversely' or 'alternatively' this time.

'EMPHASISING' DISCOURSE MARKERS

- ABOVE ALL

- IN PARTICULAR

- ESPECIALLY

- SIGNIFICANTLY

- INDEED

- NOTABLY

You can breathe a sigh of relief now! It's over! No more connectives. However, now I want to put our new found skills to use in our essays.

Useful information/Glossary

Allegory: extended metaphor, like the grim reaper representing death, e.g. Scrooge symbolizing capitalism.

Alliteration: same consonant sound repeating, e.g. 'She sells sea shells'.

Allusion: reference to another text/person/place/event.

Ascending tricolon: sentence with three parts, each increasing in power, e.g. 'ringing, drumming, shouting'.

Aside: character speaking so some characters cannot hear what is being said. Sometimes, an aside is directly to the audience. It's a dramatic technique which reveals the character's inner thoughts and feelings.

Assonance: same vowel sounds repeating, e.g. 'Oh no, won't Joe go?'

Bathos: abrupt change from sublime to ridiculous for humorous effect.

Blank verse: lines of unrhymed iambic pentameter.

Compressed time: when the narrative is fast-forwarding through the action.

Descending tricolon: sentence with three parts, each decreasing in power, e.g. 'shouting, talking, whispering'.

Denouement: tying up loose ends, the resolution.

Diction: choice of words or vocabulary.

Dilated time: opposite compressed time, here the narrative is in slow motion.

Direct address: second person narrative, predominantly using the personal pronoun 'you'.

Dramatic action verb: manifests itself in physical action, e.g. I punched him in the face.

Dramatic irony: audience knows something that the character is unaware of.

Ellipsis: leaving out part of the story and allowing the reader to fill in the narrative gap.

End-stopped lines: poetic lines that end with punctuation.

Epistolary: letter or correspondence-driven narrative.

Flashback/Analepsis: going back in time to the past, interrupting the chronological sequence.

Flashforward/Prolepsis: going forward in time to the future, interrupting the chronological sequence.

Foreshadowing/Adumbrating: suggestion of plot developments that will occur later in the narrative.

Gothic: another strand of Romanticism, typically with a wild setting, a sensitive heroine, an older man with a 'piercing gaze', discontinuous structure, doppelgangers, guilt and the 'unspeakable' (according to Eve Kosofsky Sedgwick).

Hamartia: character flaw, leading to that character's downfall.

Hyperbole: exaggeration for effect.

Iambic pentameter: a line of ten syllables beginning with a lighter stress alternating with a heavier stress in its perfect form, which sounds like a heartbeat. The stress falls on the even syllables, numbers: 2, 4, 6, 8 and 10, e.g. 'When now I think you can behold such sights'.

Intertextuality: links to other literary texts.

Irony: amusing or cruel reversal of expected outcome or words meaning the opposite to their literal meaning.

Metafiction/Romantic irony: self-conscious exposure of the devices used to create 'the truth' within a work of fiction.

Motif: recurring image use of language or idea that connects the narrative together and creates a theme or mood, e.g. 'green light' in *The Great Gatsby.*

Oxymoron: contradictory terms combined, e.g. deafening silence.

Pastiche: imitation of another's work.

Pathetic fallacy: a form of personification whereby inanimate objects show human attributes, e.g. 'the sea smiled benignly'. The originator of the term, John Ruskin in 1856, used 'the cruel, crawling foam', from Kingsley's *The Sands of Dee*, as an example to clarify what he meant by the 'morbid' nature of pathetic fallacy.

Personification: concrete or abstract object made human, often simply achieved by using a capital letter or a personal pronoun, e.g. 'Nature', or describing a ship as 'she'.

Pun/Double entendre: a word with a double meaning, usually employed in witty wordplay but not always.

Retrospective: account of events after they have occurred.

Romanticism: genre celebrating the power of imagination, spriritualism and nature.

Semantic/lexical field: related words about a single concept, e.g. king, queen and prince are all concerned with royalty.

Soliloquy: character thinks aloud, but is not heard by other characters (unlike in a monologue) giving the audience access to inner thoughts and feelings.

Style: choice of language, form and structure, and effects produced.

Synecdoche: one part of something referring to the whole, e.g. Carker's teeth represent him in *Dombey and Son*.

Syntax: the way words and sentences are placed together.

Tetracolon climax: sentence with four parts, culminating with the last part, e.g. 'I have nothing to offer but blood, toil, tears, and sweat ' (Winston Churchill).

ABOUT THE AUTHOR

Joe Broadfoot is a secondary school teacher of English and a soccer journalist, who also writes fiction and literary criticism. His former experiences as a DJ took him to far-flung places such as Tokyo, Kobe, Beijing, Hong Kong, Jakarta, Cairo, Dubai, Cannes, Oslo, Bergen and Bodo. He is now PGCE and CELTA-qualified with QTS, a first-class honours degree in Literature and an MA in Victorian Studies. Drama is close to his heart as he acted in 'Macbeth' and 'A Midsummer Night's Dream' at the Royal Northern College of Music in Manchester. More recently, he has been teaching 'Much Ado About Nothing' to 'A' Level students at a secondary school in Buckinghamshire, 'An Inspector Calls' at a school in west London and 'Heroes' at a school in Kent.

Printed in Great Britain
by Amazon